LADIES SING CHRISTMAS

CONTEMPORARY

AND TRADITIONAL

FAVORITES

ARRANGED FOR

TRIO, ENSEMBLE,

OR CHOIR

BY TOM FETTKE

LILLENAS
PUBLISHING COMPANY
Kansas City, MO 64141
LILLENAS.COM

CONTENTS

4

Go Tell It!

The Virgin Mary Had a Baby Boy
Go, Tell It on the Mountain

*Arranged by Tom Fettke
and Camp Kirkland*

ba - by boy,_____ And they said that His name was
Child is born,_____ And they said that His name was
of the world,_____ And they said that His name was

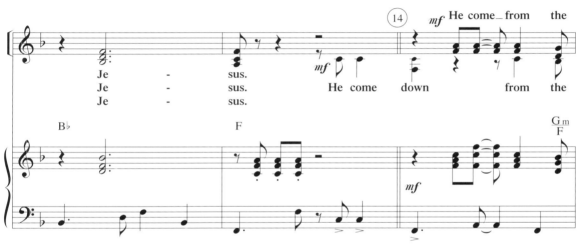

Je - sus.
Je - sus. He come down from the
Je - sus.

14 *mf* He come_ from the

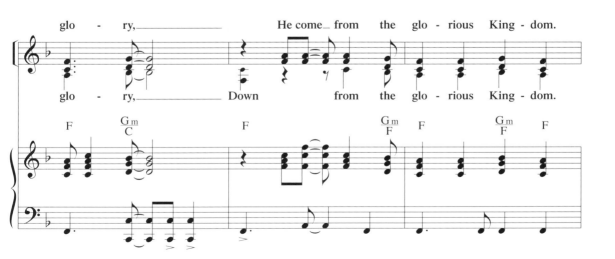

glo - ry,_____ He come_ from the glo - rious King - dom.
glo - ry,_____ Down from the glo - rious King - dom.

6

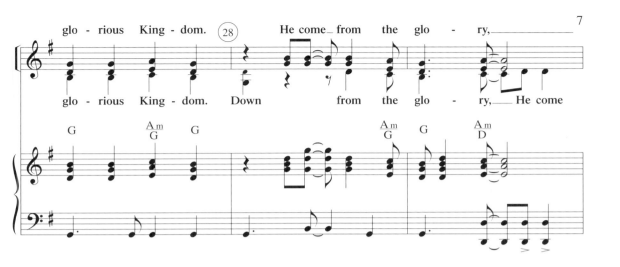

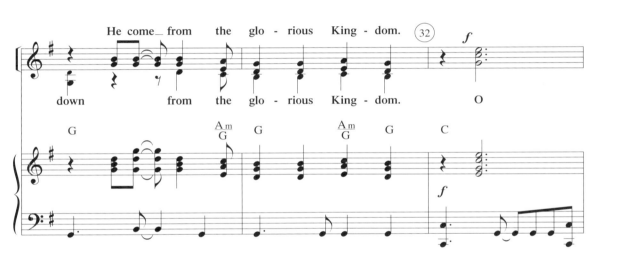

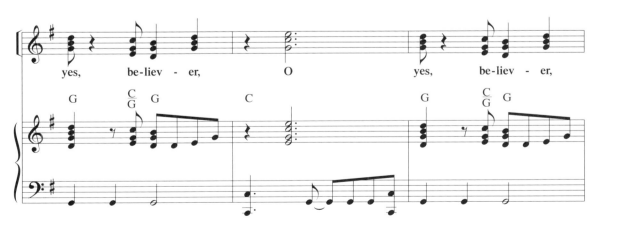

8

Precious Promise

Words and Music by
STEVEN CURTIS CHAPMAN
Arranged by Tom Fettke

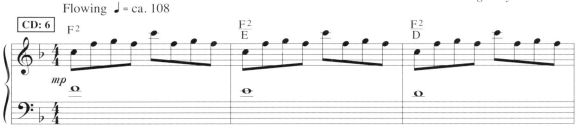

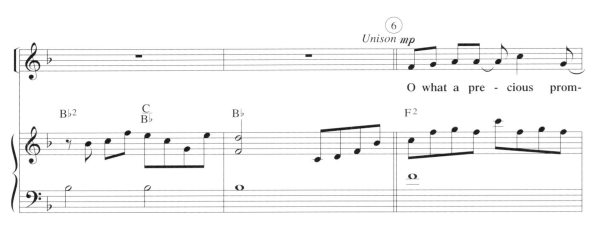

O what a pre - cious prom-

- ise, _____ O what a gift ___ of love _____ An

12

16

18

Thou Didst Leave Thy Throne

EMILY S. ELLIOTT

TIMOTHY R. MATTHEWS
Arranged by Richard Kingsmore
S.S.A. arrangement by Tom Fettke

20

*The original text is "My heart shall rejoice, Lord Jesus, when Thou comest and callest for me." This piece may be used as an invitation, so the text included in the music is more appropriate.

24

Simple Worship

with
That Beautiful Name

KEN BIBLE

TOM FETTKE
Arranged by Tom Fettke

Warmly ♩ = ca. 72

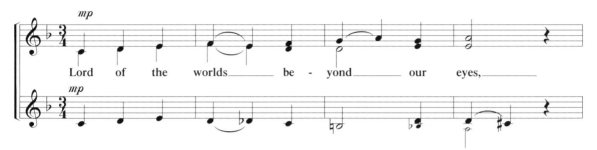

Lord of the worlds be-yond our eyes,

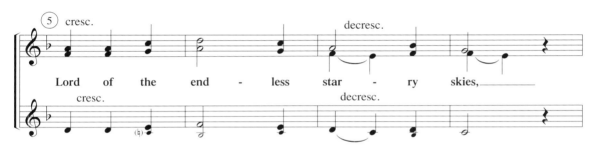

Lord of the end-less star-ry skies,

An-gels all bow to speak Your name.

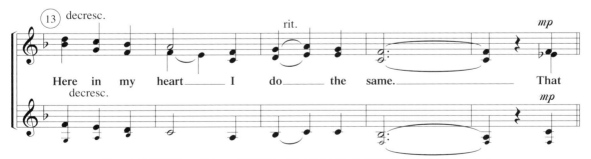

Here in my heart I do the same. That

*"That Beautiful Name"

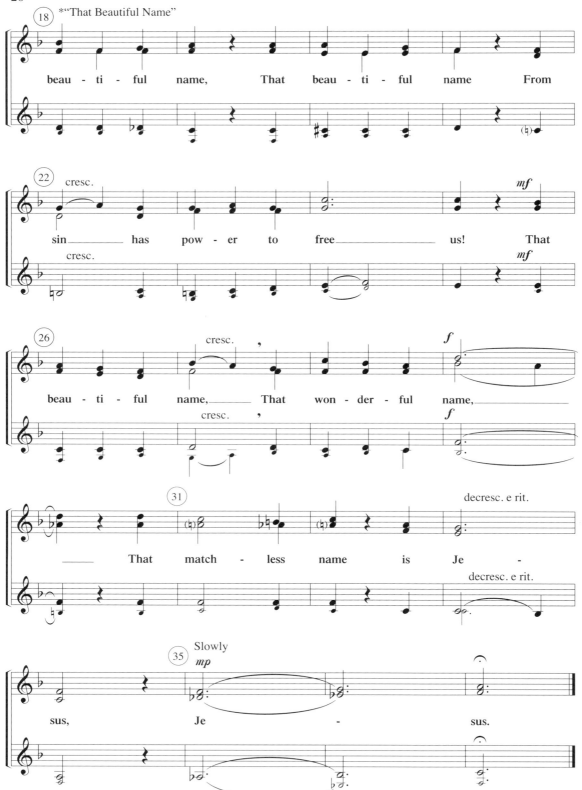

beau - ti - ful name, That beau - ti - ful name From

sin____ has pow - er to free____ us! That

beau - ti - ful name,____ That won - der - ful name,____

____ That match - less name is Je -

Slowly

sus, Je - sus.

*Words by JEAN PERRY; Music by MABEL JOHNSTON CAMP. Arr. © 2003 by Pilot Point Music(ASCAP). All rights reserved. Administered by The Copyright Company, 1025 16th Avenue South, Nashville, TN 37212.

Christmas Praise

Angels, from the Realms of Glory
Bless That Wonderful Name
Wonderful Counselor
Jesus, O What a Wonderful Child

*Arranged by Camp Kirkland
and Tom Fettke*

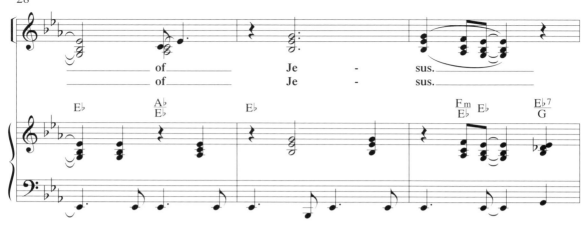

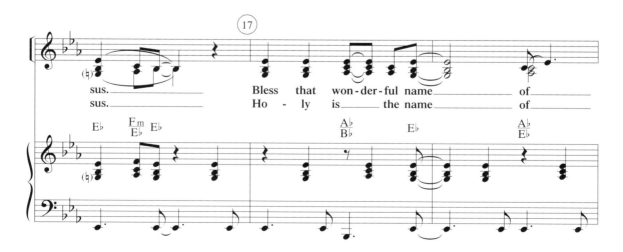

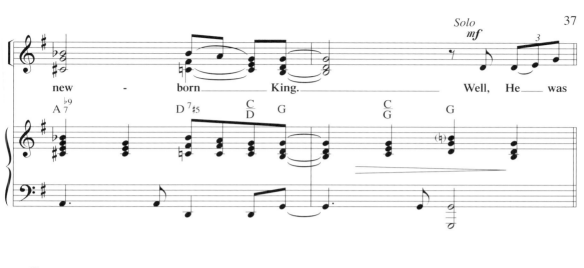

new - born King. Well, He was

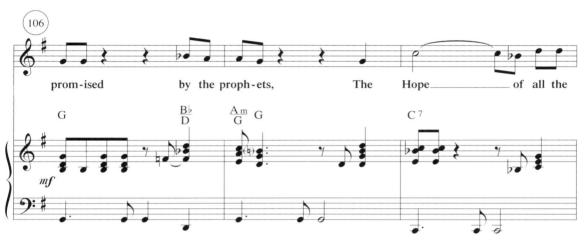

prom-ised by the proph-ets, The Hope of all the

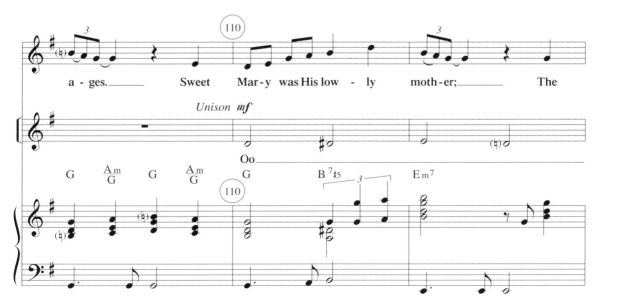

a - ges. Sweet Mar-y was His low - ly moth-er; The

38

O Lord, Most Holy

KEN BIBLE

CÉSAR FRANCK
Arranged by Tom Fettke

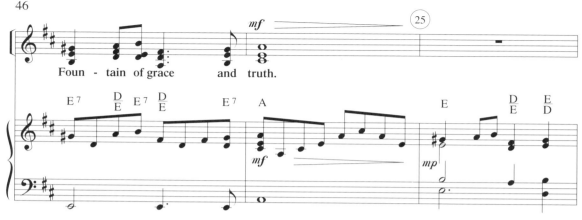

CD: 29

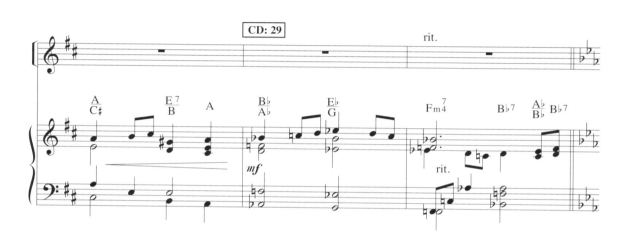

*You may wish to divide an ensemble of 4 or more into 2 equal parts for this section.

Shepherds Praise

Gloria Deo
Gloria

Arranged by Camp Kirkland
and Tom Fettke

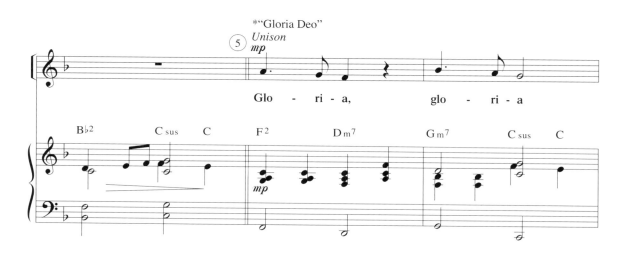

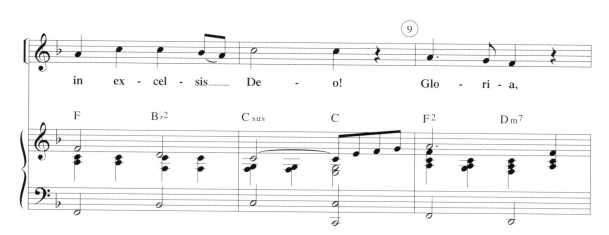

*Words, Scripture; Music by TOM FETTKE and Traditional. Copyright © 1995, and this arr. © 1995, 2003 by Pilot Point Music (ASCAP). All rights reserved. Administered by The Copyright Company, 1025 16th Avenue South, Nashville, TN 37212.

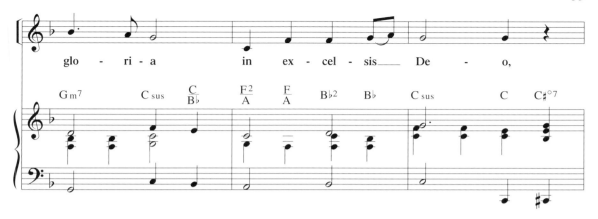

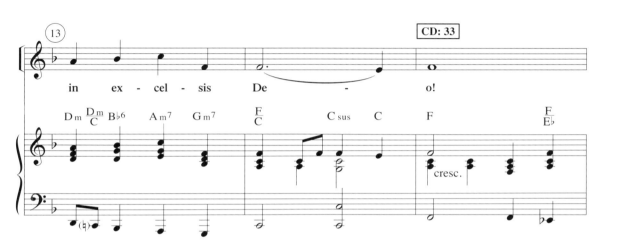

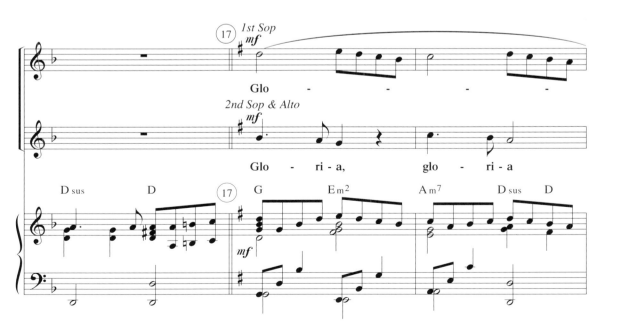

56

Both times: Solo (or unison)

King.

1. While the shep-herds in the fields watched

2. What a sound the an - gels made– the

o - ver their flocks by night, An an - gel of the Lord ap - peared with

hills just came a - live; The shep - herds were a - mazed to hear a

43

coun - te - nance so bright, An - nounc - ing they would find the Child a -

con - cert in the sky. The mes - sage that the an - gels sang was

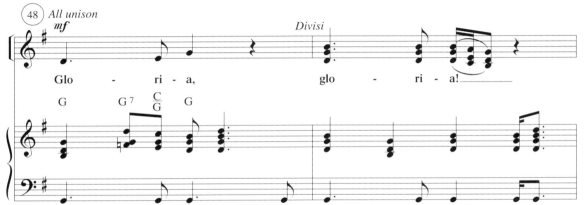

58

Saw You Never in the Twilight

CECIL F. ALEXANDER

TOM FETTKE
Arranged by Tom Fettke

1. Saw you nev - er in the twi - light,
2. Then they o - pened all their trea - sure,

When the sun had left the skies,
When they found the In - fant King,

Up in heav - en the clear stars shin - ing,
Gave Him gold and a fra - grant in - cense,

Thro' the gloom like sil - ver eyes?
Gave Him myrrh in of - fer - ing.

A Christmas Invitation

Come and See
O Come, Let Us Adore Him

Arranged by Tom Fettke

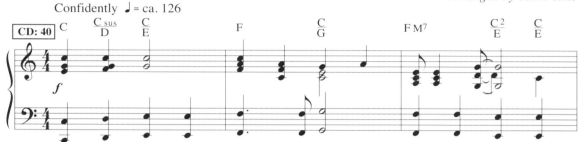

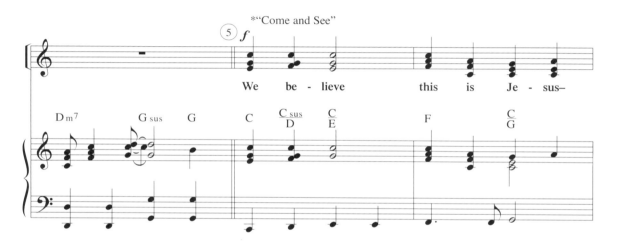

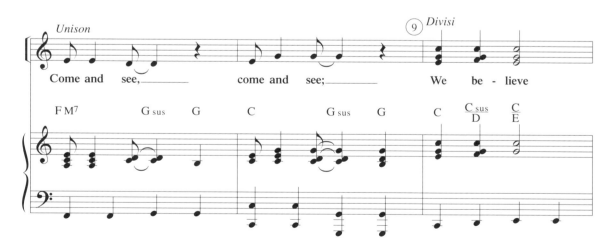

64

There Is Hope

Words and Music by
CHRISTOPHER MACHEN
Arranged by Camp Kirkland
and Tom Fettke

Lyrics:

Hope ris-es with the dawn, ris-es in the heart, shin-ing on the soul, forc-ing back the

70

72

Jesus, the Light of the World

CHARLES WESLEY and
GEORGE D. ELDERKIN

GEORGE D. ELDERKIN
Arranged by Tom Fettke

CD: 53

Child in the Manger

KEN BIBLE
and MARY MACDONALD

THOMAS J. WILLIAMS,
CAMP KIRKLAND and TOM FETTKE
Arranged by Camp Kirkland
and Tom Fettke

88

90

(to pg. 90, meas. 81)

Immanuel, Immanuel

KEN BIBLE

German Folk Song
Arranged by Tom Fettke

King of Kings Adored

Sovereign Lord
I Extol You
Holy Is the Lord

Arranged by Tom Fettke

*"I Extol You"

100 CD: 70

*Words by KEN BIBLE and Traditional; Music by FRANZ SCHUBERT. Copyright © 1998, and this arr. © 1998, 2003 by Pilot Point Music (ASCAP). All rights reserved. Administered by The Copyright Company, 1025 16th Avenue South, Nashville, TN 37212.

Hope Has Arrived

Words and Music by
REBECCA J. PECK
*Arranged by Camp Kirkland
and Tom Fettke*

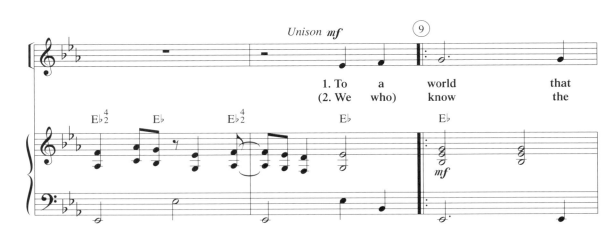

104

(to pg. 102, meas. 9)

110

Who Is This Child?

PATRICIA KING STOWELL

BENJAMIN HARLAN
Arranged by Tom Fettke

CD: 78

Come Rejoicing!

KEN BIBLE

Tattersall's *Psalmody*, 1794
Arranged by Tom Fettke

119

Come with sing - ing! Joy that's more than words can tell!

In the Son are giv - en all the gifts of heav - en!
In the Son are giv - en!

Praise His name, Em - man - u - el!

Unison

Come re - joic - ing, come re - joic - ing, come re - joic - ing, come re - joic - ing,

mp cresc. poco a poco

Divisi

come re - joic - ing, come re - joic - ing, Christ the Lord is here! Re - joice!

Emmanuel Medley

Emmanuel– Prince of Peace
His Name Is Called Emmanuel
Emmanuel

*Arranged by Camp Kirkland
and Tom Fettke*

122